Then Comes The Dawn

H J Aridan

H J Aridan

ISBN:1982077379
ISBN-13: 978-1982077372

DEDICATION

To Samantha,

my best friend,
my rock,
I would be nothing without you

and
To all the boys who broke my heart,
and the one who came to mend it.

ACKNOWLEDGMENTS

Thank you to you, the reader, for abandoning reason and absorbing
these words.
It means more than you know.

Part I

The Dark Before…

Start

i start **here**
my mouth dry
my tears,
stinging my red cheeks,
me
i
the girl you gave up
the girl you lost
                    the girl

the girl

                                        the girl

the woman...

                        i have become

Birthright

there is no such thing
as a weak Fe(male)
the first two letters
of the very word
are the element
of iron,
strength
is your
birthright

She

once

long ago
there was no you and i,
just us,
we.

                              but then

                    then there was she...

5

Release

how does it feel
looking into my eyes
when last night
yours were fixed on
her
naked
body,
warm
beneath you

you turned around,
you went back,
on your way home to me
you sought her release
instead of mine

Rejection

rejection
is like a snake bite
you have to
suck
the poison
out
in order for
you
to heal

Scared

i **am** scared
that one day
i will no longer
be afraid to
hate you

I

i am

not a writer

i think

i am

just a girl

with sadness in her heart

but fire in her soul

Temptation

being loved by a man
is so different
to being
lusted after
by a boy;

one
will see you as his reflection

         the other
         will see you
         as his temptation

Fracture

when you no longer feel the pain,
when it's so enduring
that all you feel is numb,
that's when you force yourself
to fracture;
you can heal better
from being broken
than you can
from being ignorant

Ruins

in the moments
when you feel
entirely broken
remember,
the most beautiful cities
were built
upon
ruins

Caveat

there was always a caveat
to your soul;
gentleman mixed with rogue

it was never the gentleman you showed me,
in the end,
it was only the mask of broken man

Storm

i deserve more.

the irony is,
you knew it all along.

but you kept me;
a prisoner of hope,
for no reason
other than you were broken
and i was the sunshine after your storm

Cheap

i lay in your arms
knowing
i am nothing more
than cheap thrills
and late night entertainment.
i say nothing,
hoping that one day you would see me

you didn't

Loneliness

i've decided
to embrace my loneliness
for no other reason
than the fact it is
far better
company
than you ever were

Excuses

i gave you all the excuses
all the slack
all the love
i should have given myself

Apathy

my

                                   brokenness

is not
my apathy,

it

                           is

the engine

 for

                           my

                       empathy

Truth

a real man
will tell the
truth
even when he knows
it will hurt you;
the problem is,
that they often tell you too late

Leave

go on,
leave;
like they all do,
but you'll come back;
like they all do,
you'll realise what you've lost;
like they all do;

what makes you think that i will turn
around;
just for you

Thief

my heart is a diamond
and you are its thief,
be so kind and return it,
to the more grateful owner...

Company

i don't love you,
i love your company
funny isn't it,
how one
can so often be mistaken for the other

Strangle

i don't write poetry because i can,
i write
because if i couldn't,
i would strangle myself in my own words

Three

i told you that you'd want it;
maybe not
in three weeks,
or three months,
or three years,
but by then it's too late
because i will have fallen in love
with myself,
and i am more important to me
than you will ever be

Self

i have carved a new body for myself;
for your hands moulded me,
twisted,
and contorted me,
deconstructed
and destroyed me.

i remade myself.

delicately rebuilt myself
softly and potently renewed myself
i reclaim my.
self.

you.

you have lost this self
this kind and generous
this loving self,
which you took and avenged
for your own
broken
damaged self.

don't blame yourself.

but i do.

Enemy

it was all going so well,
until you mistook my kindness
for weakness,
my passion
for desire
and you my enemy,
as my ally

Sometimes

sometimes,
i don't know which is worse;
me handing you the gun,
or you pulling the trigger

Language

i've come to realise;
that love isn't a universal language,
but heartbreak certainly is

Writers

how poignant,
that wounded writers
often find solace
in one another

Excuse

when they say

"i don't have an excuse"

what they mean is

"i knew it was wrong but I didn't stop"

Ache

i no longer ache for you,
my body now aches
in the knowledge
i chose needing you
over loving me

Sin

it's almost a shame,
that the back seat of my car
has seen more sin
than my bed ever did

History

i will never shake the feeling
that we were long lost lovers;
but,
we were better left in history

Driving

i used to find driving
such a soothing pastime;
music blaring,
windows down,
heaters on,
lips forming the words,
to my favourite songs.

but now,
every song,
reminds me of you,
and suddenly,
driving has become
a punishment
in which there is no room;

for reprieve,
since each lyric,
each melody
was interwoven
into our story
a story,
that ended too suddenly
and too ferociously
to ever be happy

Sting

trying
to hold onto someone
is like capturing a scorpion
and
praying
it doesn't sting.

there's less possibility of pain,
after
the letting go

Hurt

tell me,
how did it feel,
knowing you could hurt me,
just as quickly as you had her.

Sordid

you took my life
and made it
into your sordid affair,
fucking it
whenever you fancied

Ending

i never really wanted a happy ending;
i never wanted an ending at all

Abandonment

if only my tongue
can move in my mouth
like the way it moved in yours
maybe my words won't be swallowed
by my fear
and your abandonment

Destruction

you used me
for no reason
other than I was convenient
and you were broken

i was your healing
you were my destruction

Wondering

if you were wondering,
yes,
the last one was probably about you...

Someone

one day i will belong to someone **else**
someone **new**
someone **who understands my value**
someone **who loves me**
like you were supposed to
but what terrifies me,
truly frightens my soul,
is that if you came back
i would still say no

Losing

you were not the wind in my sails
you did not push me forward
you did not carry me
but you moved me
further away from myself
because loving you
meant losing me

enough now.

Convincing

convincing **someone to love you is easy,**
it's harder
when that someone is yourself

Woman

woman,
**you are more beautiful
more powerful
and more worthy,
than the feeling of his hands
on your thighs**

Name

to all the girls
boys
men
women,

the lonely souls
the broken hearts

the ones crying themselves to sleep

you are worthy

your battle cry is your name

say it

own it

there is value

in the letters of your being

Part II

The Dawn

Reborn

and silently
as the last breath of summer
oozed its warmth into the world,
one final time.
she found herself reborn

Ready

consume me,
my soul
is ready
for the taking

Reality

i knew it was you
from the moment we first met
i knew you were the man
not of my
dreams
but of my reality
and you
were so much better
than all of my fantasies
put together

Versions

there are versions,
of the same story.
of your story.
you have the pen

please begin writing.

Chemical

"it's chemical;
love.
it is merely a reaction in the brain,
nothing more,
nothing less.
it is biology."

oh but my dear,
i have come to learn
it can be so much more

Coffee

consume me like how you drink coffee.

my bitterness overshadowed by the vibrancy.
of my body;
my aroma drawing you in like warm shelter
from a raging storm;
a sip of my warmth,
the bursting of my taste on your tongue;
my strength not defined by numbers
but by the flavour that pours out of me;
pour me into you.
you'll see how sweet i can be.

Strength

i do not fear my weakness
i fear my own strength;

one can be tamed

the other is a beast

waiting

to be unleashed

Stroke

like an artist
with every stroke
you paint me,
with colour
bursting
from my soul,
turning the blank walls
of my bedroom
into a canvas
that captures
every delicious moan
you command from my body.

Fire

you set my soul on fire
and i sat there
and i let myself burn

Numb

you taught me
what it means
to feel
when all i felt

was numb

Inconvenience

i find sleep an inconvenience,
the days are too short,
the nights even shorter,
there is too much to be done in such little
time.

i never liked the moon anyway...

Something

i have fought through this life
with the unshakable
feeling that something
something
something
something
was missing.

it turns out
it was you all along

Joy

there is no greater image
than the smile
that sits on your lips
parting the way
for your joy
to escape

and

                    find

                                        me

Beautiful

don't tell me
that i'm beautiful;
tell me
that i'm brilliant,
my looks will eventually fade,
but my essence will never diminish

Greedy

greedy.
if you want to know
how i feel for you,
i am greedy.
not for your touch
or for your lips on my neck
or for your fingers,
dancing,
down my spine
like they do.
you,
i am greedy **for you**
for your mind
for your soul
for your heart.
i am
unashamedly
greedy.

Music

you.
you are the harmony
the melody
the perfect 7th
my resolution.

you are music
i am yours,
let me show you
how i can sing

Dreamer

"you are every star in my sky.
you are the dreamer,
the believer,
the dancer of my thoughts,
the singer of my soul.
you are the light of my life"

she says, looking in a mirror.

Equal

he was not my

master,

he was my

equal;

he dipped his head,

arose

from *his*

alter

and knelt before his queen

Softly

softly,
you trace your fingers
over my skin
and i count the seconds
until i am lost
between your thumb
and the palm of your hand

Witness

i healed myself
and you were there
just in time
to witness
the salvation

Entrance

you made your entrance
without warning.
i didn't see you coming
but i could feel you missing,
ironic isn't it
that my soul missed you
before i knew i could

Worthy

as the cerulean skies glitter
through the frost bitten morning,
i am reminded
that everything
that is worthy of new growth,
had to decay first

Honey

honey
my name drips,
thick and viscous like
honey
from your lips
a benediction,
a prayer,
a plea.

Mornings

if i close my eyes,
i can;
still hear you breathe,
i can;
still feel the faint rise and fall
of your body next to me,
i can;
still feel your heat reaching out
to soothe my frost bitten feet,
i can;
still feel your heart racing
as you had me,
pinned
beneath your desire,
and our fires,
mingling
like hot breath
on the iciest of mornings

Swim

let me swim in you,
dive into your soul
float in your being
let me feel your waves,
your undulations,
i want all of me,
surrounded by all of you

Rise

rise, **girl;**
rise with conviction in your heart,
fire in your soul,
and kindness in your eyes

Slow

slow,
so
slow
my name
on your tongue
like my body was
moments before,
soft
yet purposeful

Embers

and i swore in that moment
that no ice
would ever swallow the fire
that rages on inside of me,
flames
lapping at my fingertips
embers falling at my feet

Volumes

volumes
**are spoken
of women
who remain silent
in their pain.**

**their anguish,
their fire
and their souls...**

what of their souls?

**their souls,
set ablaze by the men
who lost them,
can engulf even the iciest
of hearts.**

Discover

in such little time
i have learnt your body,
i have learnt the things
that make you tense,
i have learnt the things
that are your undoing,
i have learnt,
and i
will continue to learn
what it means
to explore
and discover
and claim,
your land
as my own.

Lesson

you are a lesson.
all of you,
every inch of skin
each undulation of muscle,
you are a lesson
that I will never
tire of

Beauty

when will we stop teaching young women
that beauty is painted onto a face,
when really,
they're covering infinite beauty with a
finite mask

Devour

if i am a star
you must be the whole universe
go ahead,
devour **me**

Chaos

they say there is no order to chaos;
yet here i stand,
ordering you to love me.

Breathe

breathe.
remember you are worthy
you have great value
even when you don't believe it,
i see you

Dance

i have waited
more years than you know
to dance
with you
in my living room,
in complete silence.
the only sound
our feet on the marble floor,

who needs an accompaniment
when you and i are the music

Piano

you.
sat at my piano,
music.
flowing,
around me.
finally,
my soul felt happy.

Happy

i realised,
the second you smiled at me,
that i wanted to lose myself
in your happy

Only

the only person
i have ever
truly sought love from
was myself

Ocean

smile, darling
because you are the tide
and he is just a grain of sand
in the ocean
that you control

Endured

the hardest lesson
i have endured
is learning how
to love myself for my mind;
learning,
that i don't need attention
nor affection,
from those
who refuse to see
past my body;
accepting myself for me,
for who i have become,
not for who they perceive me to be,

that
is

the hardest lesson
i have endured

Sunday

it was a sunday morning
snow falling
languidly
like how
your fingers
soothe my body.
and in that moment
i was glad you couldn't leave.

Please

i will never forget
the moment
your hands
pressed mine into the mattress,
and i whispered,

"please."

Whiskey

like whiskey
on my tongue
i still taste
you
even when you are gone

Dawn

you
you are the dawn
i
i am your shelter
rest in me
whilst i bask in your warmth

Fear

fear **the broken woman**

for when she heals

her strength

can destroy more

than when you tried to destroy her

Eden

we

are

the

beginning

The ~~End~~
Start
Is
Now

26351701R00055

Printed in Great Britain
by Amazon